ZENTRIC ALCHEMY

TRANSFORMING COMPLEXITY INTO ENTREPRENEURIAL GOLD

By

CA MOHIT MAKKAR

About The Author 

CA Mohit Makkar is not just a Chartered Accountant—he is a strategist, mentor, and problem solver for businesses navigating the complexities of the Indian financial landscape. With over 22 years of experience in **Auditing, Taxation, Commercial Laws, and Statutory Compliance**, he has worked closely with entrepreneurs, guiding them through financial challenges and regulatory hurdles.

As the **founding partner of MVM & Associates**, he has played a crucial role in helping businesses optimize their tax structures, strengthen internal controls, and ensure compliance with ever-evolving legal frameworks. His expertise extends across **direct and indirect taxation, SEBI regulations, GST advisory, forensic accounting, and corporate law matters**, making him a trusted advisor for individuals and businesses alike.

Throughout his career, Mohit has witnessed firsthand the **struggles, missteps, and triumphs** of Indian entrepreneurs. This book is a result of that experience—**a practical guide to navigating the intricate financial and legal challenges that every business owner faces**. His goal is simple: to break down complex problems and provide actionable solutions that empower entrepreneurs to build sustainable and compliant businesses.

Beyond his professional achievements, Mohit is an avid **cricket enthusiast and passionate reader. He believes** that a well-rounded life fosters creativity and resilience—two essential traits for any entrepreneur.

Through this book, he hopes to **demystify financial and regulatory challenges, inspire entrepreneurs to make informed decisions, and ultimately contribute to the success stories of India's business ecosystem**.

PREFACE

In today's dynamic business environment, running a company in India is **both an opportunity and a challenge**. Entrepreneurs and business leaders must navigate an ever-evolving maze of **regulatory requirements, taxation policies, financial planning, and operational complexities**—all while ensuring their organizations remain competitive and future-ready.

Over the past two decades as a **Chartered Accountant and business advisor**, I have had the privilege of working with **start-ups, SMEs, and large corporations** across diverse industries.

A common theme I have observed is that **many business owners struggle with financial and legal intricacies**, often making **avoidable mistakes that lead to compliance risks, financial inefficiencies, and operational bottlenecks**.

This book is my attempt to bridge that knowledge gap. It is **not a technical manual filled with legal jargon** but rather a **practical guide designed to provide clear, actionable insights** for business leaders.

Whether you are:

- **An aspiring entrepreneur** setting up a new venture

- **A seasoned business owner** looking to strengthen financial and regulatory compliance

- **A financial professional** seeking deeper insights into taxation, auditing, and statutory obligations

...this book is structured to help you **understand, implement, and sustain best practices** in business operations, compliance, and financial management.

What makes this book different is its **real-world approach**—instead of merely outlining legal clauses, it focuses on **how to apply them effectively in your business**. It covers **common pitfalls, proactive strategies, and case studies** to help you navigate challenges with confidence.

As you go through these pages, I encourage you to **think beyond compliance**—to use this knowledge as a tool for **business growth, efficiency, and long-term success.**

The goal is not just to **avoid penalties** but to **optimize processes, leverage automation, and build a resilient organization** that thrives in an ever-changing landscape.

Thank you for taking the time to explore this book. I hope it serves as a **valuable resource** and helps you **build a business that is not just compliant but also competitive, efficient, and future-proof**.

Mohit Makkar

March 2025

(Practicing Chartered Accountant & Author)

ACKNOWLEDGMENTS 

Every book is a journey, not just for the writer but also for the people who shape, inspire, and support the process along the way. This book would not have been possible without the unwavering encouragement, guidance, and belief of those who have stood by me in this endeavor.

A Mentor's Guiding Light

I extend my deepest gratitude to my mentor and coach, **Mr. Gaurav Arora**, whose invaluable wisdom, steadfast guidance, and faith in my potential have been instrumental in shaping my professional and personal growth. His insights have challenged me to think beyond limitations, turning obstacles into opportunities. This book is, in many ways, a reflection of the knowledge and discipline he has instilled in me, and I am forever grateful for his unwavering support.

The Backbone of My Journey – My Family

No words can fully express my appreciation for my **beloved wife, Saru Makkar, and my dear son, Shanjan Makkar**. Their boundless love, patience, and encouragement have been my greatest strength. Through long hours, endless revisions, and moments of self-doubt, they stood beside me, offering unwavering support. Their belief in me has been the fuel that kept me going, making this journey not just possible but deeply meaningful.

I also owe a profound debt of gratitude to my **parents and parents-in-law**, whose blessings, love, and values have been the foundation of my aspirations. Their lessons on perseverance, integrity, and resilience have shaped the person I am today. Their unwavering faith in my abilities has been a source of strength, pushing me to strive for excellence in all my endeavors.

The Strength of a Dedicated Team

To my **colleagues and team members**, thank you for stepping up and taking on additional responsibilities in my absence. Your dedication, resilience, and teamwork ensured that our shared goals remained on track, and your commitment has been nothing short of inspiring. It is an honor to work alongside such a devoted and hardworking team, and I deeply appreciate your support in making this book a reality.

Bringing Stories to Life

A special note of appreciation goes to **Mrs. Shveta Gupta and Mrs. Ritu Nakra**, whose insightful contributions have enriched this book with real-world perspectives. The scenarios and experiences they shared have added depth, making the content more practical and relatable. Their thoughtful input has helped bridge the gap between theoretical knowledge and everyday business challenges, making this work not just informative but also deeply human.

A Collective Achievement

This book is not just my effort—it is the result of the encouragement, wisdom, and contributions of all those who have been a part of this journey. To each of you, **thank you for believing in me, for sharing your knowledge, and for being my pillars of strength**. Your support has made this book possible, and I dedicate this work to the invaluable role you have played in my life.

Mohit Makkar

(Practicing Chartered Accountant & Author)

TABLE OF CONTENTS

CHAPTER 1

COMPLIANCES AND REGULATORY FRAMEWORK AND SOLUTIONS FOR ENTREPRENEURS

1. Challenges and Complexities

Starting a business in India can be an exciting journey, but it also comes with its fair share of challenges. As a chartered accountant, I have seen many entrepreneurs struggle with understanding the many compliances and regulations that are part of launching a business. This book is intended to demystify the process, breaking down complex procedures into simple, understandable steps. Whether you are choosing a legal structure or completing multiple registrations, this guide will help you navigate the process with confidence.

1.1 Choosing the Right Legal Structure

One of the biggest hurdles for any entrepreneur is selecting the appropriate legal structure for their venture. Options include:

- **Private Limited Company**

- **Limited Liability Partnership (LLP)**

- **Sole Proprietorship**

Choosing the right legal structure is a critical decision for any entrepreneur, as it not only shapes daily operations but also influences long-term business growth and risk management. For example, a Private Limited Company provides a formal framework that includes limited liability protection, thereby safeguarding personal assets; however, this structure entails more stringent regulatory compliance and higher administrative overhead. In contrast, a Limited Liability Partnership (LLP) combines elements of partnership flexibility with the benefit of limited liability, offering a balance between operational freedom and risk mitigation while still requiring adherence to certain legal formalities. Meanwhile, a Sole Proprietorship offers the simplest setup and ease of management but places the owner at risk of unlimited personal liability, which can affect financial security in adverse situations. Each option presents unique advantages and challenges that must be carefully considered in relation to your business goals, financial planning, and risk appetite.

1.2 Comparison of Legal Structures: LLP, Private Limited Company, and Proprietorship

When selecting the appropriate legal structure for a business, it is essential to understand the key differences among Limited Liability Partnerships (LLPs), Private Limited Companies, and Proprietorships. LLPs offer a hybrid structure that combines the operational flexibility of partnerships with the advantage of limited liability, making them suitable for professional services and collaborative ventures. Private Limited Companies, on the other hand, are separate legal entities that require a more formalized corporate governance framework and stringent compliance measures, which can enhance credibility and attract investor funding. In contrast, Proprietorships are the simplest form of business with minimal regulatory burdens, but they expose the owner to unlimited personal liability. The following comparison outlines these differences in terms of legal structure, liability, governance, compliance, taxation, and overall suitability, providing a clear guide to help entrepreneurs choose the most appropriate framework based on their business goals and risk appetite.

Aspect	Limited Liability Partnership (LLP)	Private Limited Company	Proprietorship
Legal Structure	A hybrid structure governed by the LLP Act, 2008 combines features of both partnerships and companies.	Separate legal entity incorporated under the Companies Act, 2013.	Simplest business form, owned and operated by a single individual, not a separate legal entity.
Liability	Limited liability protection for partners.	Liability is limited to the amount invested in the share capital by the shareholders.	Unlimited liability; the proprietor is personally responsible for all business obligations and debts.

Governance	Flexible internal management with minimal formalities; partners can decide operational structures without rigid corporate protocols.	Requires a formal board of directors, regular meetings, and adherence to strict statutory requirements such as annual returns, financial audits, and corporate governance norms.	Minimal formalities; the proprietor makes all decisions and manages the business independently.
Compliance	It requires annual filings with the MCA (e.g., Statement of Accounts and Solvency) and other statutory obligations, but it is generally less stringent than those for a Private Limited Company.	High regulatory and disclosure obligations, including regular filings with the MCA, holding board meetings, and maintaining detailed records in compliance with corporate laws.	Lower regulatory burden with fewer mandatory filings and less stringent compliance requirements.
Taxation	Taxed as a partnership; profits are taxed in the hands of the partners.	Subject to corporate tax on profits, dividends may be taxed at the shareholder level.	Income is taxed as the personal income of the proprietor.
Suitability	Ideal for professional services and businesses	Preferred by businesses aiming for growth,	Best suited for small-scale businesses or startups with

	seeking operational flexibility combined with limited liability protection.	attracting investor funding, and enhancing credibility among stakeholders.	low-risk exposure and minimal capital requirements.

This table provides a concise comparison of the three legal structures under current legal enactments. It is recommended that you consult with legal and tax professionals to determine the most suitable structure based on your specific business needs and circumstances.

1.3 Multiple Registrations and Compliances

Once you have chosen a legal structure, the next step is to get registered with various government bodies. In India, entrepreneurs must complete several registration processes, which include but are not limited to:

- **Tax Compliances:**

  - **Goods and Services Tax (GST) registration:** Essential for businesses that exceed the prescribed turnover threshold.

  - **TAN (Tax Deduction and Collection Account Number):** Required for businesses responsible for deducting tax at source.

  - **PAN (Permanent Account Number):** A mandatory identification number for financial transactions

- **Employee-Related Compliances:**

  - **Registration under the Employee State Insurance (ESI):** Applicable for organizations employing a certain number of workers, ensuring benefits under the ESI scheme.

  - **Registration under the Provident Fund (PF) scheme is** necessary for businesses where the scheme is applicable, safeguarding employee retirement funds.

- **Financial & Statutory Compliances:**

  - **Annual audits:** A requisite process to ensure transparent financial reporting.

  - **Statutory filings with the Registrar of Companies (ROC) and income tax authorities:** Mandatory submissions with the Registrar of Companies (ROC) and income tax authorities to maintain legal and regulatory standing.

- **IT and Data Protection:**

  - **Compliance with the Information Technology Act:** Ensures adherence to legal requirements for digital operations.

  - **Adhering to data privacy and cybersecurity norms:** Critical for protecting sensitive information and maintaining trust.

Each of these registrations involves different processes and may require guidance from various consultants—legal, tax, and financial experts. This fragmented approach often creates confusion and delays, adding to the overall challenge for the entrepreneur.

1.4 The One-Stop Government Initiative

Recognizing the inherent complexities of the registration process, the government has introduced an integrated one-stop solution aimed at streamlining compliance for entrepreneurs. For those opting for legal structures such as an LLP or a Company, this platform facilitates the completion of most, if not all, mandatory registration and compliance procedures in a single interface. This eliminates the need for multiple visits to various government offices and deals with disparate agencies for each registration. Designed to reduce bureaucratic hurdles significantly, this unified approach not only saves valuable time but also allows business owners to concentrate on strategic growth and core operational activities, thereby enhancing overall efficiency and compliance management.

1.5 Leveraging Digital Tools and Automation

After completing the initial legal registration, the next step is to ensure ongoing compliance. Modern digital tools and automated systems can help manage:

- **Regular Filing Requirements:** Automation provides timely reminders and facilitates seamless filings for tax returns, GST, and other statutory submissions, ensuring deadlines are consistently met.

- **Accounting Systems:** Cloud-based accounting solutions simplify financial record-keeping and reporting, reducing manual errors and enhancing transparency.

- **Data Protection:** Advanced digital solutions help maintain adherence to IT regulations and data protection standards, safeguarding sensitive information against breaches.

These tools not only reduce the likelihood of human error but also enable entrepreneurs to stay updated with evolving regulatory changes.

1.6 Additional Government Support

Entrepreneurs can also benefit from other government initiatives such as:

- **Startup India:** This initiative provides a host of incentives, including grants and subsidies, to reduce regulatory burdens and foster innovation, thereby making it easier for new ventures to thrive.

- **MSME Registration Framework:** Tailored for small and medium enterprises, this framework simplifies compliance processes while offering access to financial benefits and other support services, enabling businesses to scale efficiently.

These programs are instrumental in promoting a favorable business environment and encouraging entrepreneurial success.

- **Access to Expert Guidance**

Even with streamlined processes and digital solutions, expert guidance remains a cornerstone of sustained compliance and strategic decision-making. Engaging with professionals who specialize in corporate law, taxation, and labor regulations can help ensure that your business adheres to all statutory requirements while avoiding costly errors. As a chartered accountant, I advise entrepreneurs to simplify compliance by embracing a one-stop solution. By choosing a legal structure such as an LLP or a Company, you can consolidate multiple registrations and filings under a single platform, thereby reducing the administrative burden. Furthermore, leveraging advanced digital tools and automation for tax filings, statutory submissions, and data protection can significantly decrease manual errors and enhance overall operational efficiency. This streamlined approach not only minimizes bureaucratic challenges but also enables you to focus on driving growth and fostering innovation.

BUILDING A STRONG TEAM

"Great things in business are never done by one person; they're done by a team of people."

– Steve Jobs.

A strong team is the foundation of a successful business. No matter how brilliant your business idea is, its execution depends on the people who bring it to life.

Many entrepreneurs struggle with hiring and retaining the right talent, particularly when competing with larger firms that offer attractive salary packages and perks. However, building a successful team is about more than just hiring the right people—it's about creating an environment where they can thrive.

As a **chartered accountant**, I have observed that businesses that invest in their people—through clear communication, recognition, and development opportunities—create a culture of trust and loyalty.

This not only enhances productivity but also builds a resilient organization that grows through collective commitment and shared success.

Challenges in Building a Strong Team

1. Finding the Right Talent

Attracting skilled professionals is difficult, especially for startups competing with established firms offering higher salaries and better benefits.

2. Ensuring Cultural Fit

A great hire isn't just about skills—it's also about alignment with company values. A poor cultural fit can lead to conflicts, low morale, and high turnover rates.

3. Limited Resources

Small businesses often have budget constraints that limit their ability to offer competitive compensation, making it harder to attract top-tier talent.

4. Unclear Roles and Responsibilities

Without clearly defined job roles, team members can experience confusion, inefficiency, and frustration, impacting overall productivity.

5. Keeping the Team Motivated

Retention is as critical as hiring. If employees feel undervalued, overworked, or see no growth prospects, they may seek opportunities elsewhere.

Strategic Solutions for Building a Resilient Team

1. Develop a Clear Hiring Plan

- Define the **skills, experience, and personality traits** needed for each role.

- Use structured interviews to assess both **technical expertise and cultural fit**.

- Leverage **employee referrals** and professional networks to find quality candidates.

2. Invest in Training and Growth

- Offer **online courses, mentorship programs, and on-the-job training** to upskill employees.

- Encourage participation in **industry conferences and certifications** to enhance expertise.

- Provide **career progression opportunities** to keep employees engaged and motivated.

3. Foster a Positive Work Environment

- Promote **open communication** where employees feel heard and valued.

- Conduct **regular team check-ins** to address concerns and ensure alignment with company goals.

- Create a **feedback-driven culture** that acknowledges contributions and encourages growth.

4. Consider Flexible Compensation Options

- In addition to salaries, explore **performance-based incentives, bonuses, and profit-sharing**.

- Offer **flexible work schedules** or remote work options to enhance job satisfaction.

- Provide **equity participation** to give employees a sense of ownership in the business.

5. Build Trust and Team Spirit

- Organize **team-building activities** to strengthen interpersonal relationships.

- Foster **collaboration through cross-functional projects** that encourage shared learning.

- Celebrate milestones, achievements, and personal successes to boost morale.

Hiring the right people is just the first step—retaining and nurturing them is what truly builds a strong, high-performing team.

By creating a supportive and engaging workplace, businesses can ensure **long-term employee commitment, increased productivity, and sustainable growth**.

Investing in people isn't just an HR strategy; it's a business imperative. A motivated and aligned team will always be your greatest asset.

CHAPTER 3

CHALLENGES OF FUNDS AND CASH FLOW MANAGEMENT DURING EXPANSION

In recent years, India's economy has witnessed unprecedented growth, opening up **new opportunities for business expansion**. Entrepreneurs are venturing into new markets, diversifying their product and service offerings, and scaling their operations. However, with expansion comes the **critical challenge of securing adequate funding and managing cash flow effectively**. Without proper financial planning, even the most promising businesses can struggle with liquidity constraints, operational inefficiencies, and increased financial risks.

3.1 Challenges in Acquiring Funds During the Expansion

3.1.1 Limited Access to Capital Markets

Many Indian small and medium enterprises face significant challenges when attempting to access capital markets. Unlike well-established multinationals, emerging businesses often struggle to meet the rigorous listing criteria. Moreover, they frequently encounter difficulties in finding reputable consultancy firms that can offer sound professional advice for capital market listings. As a result, these businesses tend to rely more heavily on traditional bank loans, which are generally more accessible compared to the complex processes involved in capital market fundraising.

3.1.2 Stringent Lending Norms

Financial institutions tend to exercise caution when extending credit to expanding businesses without a well-established record of profitability. High interest rates, strict collateral requirements, and lengthy approval processes can delay or even derail expansion plans. Additionally, fluctuations in macroeconomic indicators—such as interest rate hikes by the Reserve Bank of India—can further complicate access to necessary funds, making it even more challenging for these businesses to secure timely financing.

3.1.3 Inadequate Financial Documentation

Many growing businesses, particularly closely held family enterprises and traditional setups, often lack the level of financial transparency found in established corporations. The absence of detailed, audited financial statements and a proven track record can result in unfavorable funding terms or even lead to outright rejection by financial institutions. This lack of robust documentation undermines the confidence of potential lenders and investors, thereby limiting access to much-needed capital.

3.1.4 Alternative Funding from Close Relatives

In situations where formal financial channels are less accessible, many Indian businessmen turn to informal funding sources, such as loans from family and friends, to meet immediate liquidity requirements. Although these arrangements provide quick access to capital, they are frequently accompanied by challenges such as higher interest rates and the absence of standardized repayment frameworks. During income tax assessments, these transactions undergo rigorous scrutiny—bank statements, income tax returns, and the overall financial capacity of the lender are thoroughly reviewed to ensure credibility. This meticulous evaluation, while necessary to mitigate risk, may discourage potential lenders due to anticipated regulatory complications and adverse tax implications, ultimately reducing the availability of this critical funding source.

3.2 Challenges of cash flow management in expanding business

3.2.1 Working Capital Constraints

Expansion initiatives—such as launching new operations, increasing inventory levels, or hiring additional staff—require a steady inflow of cash. A misalignment between expenditures and income can lead to liquidity issues that, if not properly managed, may disrupt daily operations. This challenge is further compounded by prolonged delays in receivables from trade partners and government contracts, making efficient working capital management critical for Indian businesses.

3.2.2 Seasonality and Market Fluctuations

Many sectors in India, including agriculture, retail, and tourism, are subject to seasonal variations. During off-peak periods, cash inflows may decline while fixed costs remain unchanged, potentially leading to cash shortages. Accurate forecasting and strategic planning for these cycles are essential to prevent liquidity crises during critical periods.

3.2.3 Rising Operational Costs

As businesses expand, operational costs tend to increase due to factors such as higher rental expenses, rising labor costs, and greater expenditures for regulatory compliance. Regional cost variations and unexpected expenses can further strain cash reserves. Additionally, inflationary pressures can erode profit margins unless pricing strategies and cost control measures are adequately adjusted.

3.2.4 Managing Receivables and Payables

Maintaining a healthy cash flow in an expanding business requires effective management of receivables and payables. Delays in customer payments, combined with stringent credit terms from suppliers, can create a working capital gap. The solution often lies in negotiating improved terms, enforcing timely collections, and exploring options like invoice financing to bridge any gaps.

3.2.5 Unforeseen Economic and Regulatory Changes

India's dynamic economic landscape and evolving regulatory framework introduce additional risks. Sudden policy changes, shifts in taxation, or new compliance requirements can disrupt cash flow. For instance, the introduction of new GST regulations or amendments to labor laws may necessitate unplanned expenditures, thereby impacting the overall financial stability of an expanding enterprise.

3.3 Solutions and strategic approach to mitigate funding and cash flow Challenges

3.3.1 Strengthening Market Position for Capital Markets

Invest in robust accounting systems and conduct regular audits to generate reliable financial statements. Such transparency not only boosts credibility with investors but also helps in meeting stringent listing criteria. Engaging reputable financial advisors and capital market consultants early in the expansion process is also advisable to navigate compliance and listing requirements effectively.

3.3.2 Enhancing Creditworthiness and Diversifying Financing Solutions

Registering as an MSME can facilitate access to bank loans through dedicated government initiatives that offer support and even serve as guarantors. Building a strong credit history through consistent profitability and timely repayment of existing debts further reinforces your borrowing profile. While traditional bank loans remain important, exploring alternative financing avenues—such as venture capital, private equity, or structured debt—can reduce dependency on high-interest, collateral-intensive loans, thereby providing greater flexibility and more favorable terms for business growth.

3.3.3 Formalizing Financial Documentation

Adopt standardized financial documentation practices that comply with international accounting standards. This includes comprehensive reporting and regular audits to present a transparent financial picture to potential lenders and investors. Additionally, utilizing advanced financial management software can streamline record-keeping and enhance transparency, benefiting both internal reviews and external audits.

3.3.4 Structuring Informal Funding Channels

When relying on loans from family or close associates, it is essential to formalize these arrangements through clear, written agreements that specify interest rates, repayment schedules, and any collateral requirements. Proper documentation that meets regulatory standards not only minimizes risks and potential disputes but also ensures that these transactions can withstand scrutiny during tax assessments.

3.3.5 Enhancing Cash Flow Forecasting and Budgeting

Develop multiple cash flow forecasting models that simulate various economic scenarios to identify potential risks and plan appropriate mitigation strategies. Leveraging historical data, market trends, and predictive analytics can result in more accurate forecasts and realistic target-setting. Furthermore, creating a flexible budgeting framework allows for real-time adjustments to address unexpected cash flow disruptions.

3.3.6 Strengthening Negotiation Capabilities

Effective cash flow management often hinges on negotiating favorable terms with suppliers and customers. Securing long-term supply or purchase agreements can stabilize cash flows, while offering incentives—

such as discounts for early invoice payments—can enhance liquidity. Proactively renegotiating payment terms and engaging suppliers to extend payment periods can better align outgoing expenses with incoming cash flows.

3.3.7 Risk Management and Contingency Planning

Given the uncertainties associated with expansion, robust risk management practices are crucial. Maintain a contingency fund to absorb unexpected expenses or revenue shortfalls and consider appropriate business insurance policies or financial hedging strategies to protect against economic volatility. Continuous monitoring of key financial indicators and regular reassessment of cash flow forecasts will help in the early identification and mitigation of emerging risks.

CHAPTER 4

SETTING CLEAR GOALS – ALIGNING THE TEAM WITH ORGANIZATIONAL OBJECTIVES

In today's fast-paced business environment, **setting clear, strategic goals** is crucial for an organization's success. Over the years, I've observed how businesses—despite having talented teams—struggle to scale due to a lack of well-defined objectives. In one instance, a company with strong market potential faced continuous inefficiencies because its employees lacked direction. Without clear goals, workflows became disorganized, benchmarks were missed, and overall growth stagnated.

For Indian businesses facing **market volatility, competitive pressures, and evolving regulations**, a structured approach to goal-setting can drive performance and long-term sustainability. Below are key strategies to ensure goal alignment and organizational success.

4.1.1 Define Organizational Objectives

A well-articulated **vision and mission** serve as the foundation of an organization's strategic planning. A clear vision outlines the company's long-term aspirations, while a mission statement defines its core purpose and values. These elements **guide decision-making** and ensure that every team member understands the bigger picture.

Breaking long-term objectives into **smaller, actionable goals** provides clarity and motivation. When employees see how their tasks contribute to the larger mission, it **enhances engagement and productivity**. This approach also promotes **better communication and alignment**, ensuring that everyone is working towards a common objective.

4.1.2 Create Specific, Measurable Goals

Using the **SMART framework**—ensuring goals are **Specific, Measurable, Achievable, Relevant, and Time-bound**—enhances clarity and accountability.

For instance, instead of setting a vague target like *"increase sales,"* a SMART goal would be: *"Increase sales by 15% over the next quarter through targeted marketing campaigns."* This provides a clear **direction, timeline, and measurable outcome**, making it easier to track progress and adjust strategies accordingly.

4.1.3 Ensure Alignment and Communication

Once objectives are defined, they must be **communicated effectively across all levels** of the organization. A strong alignment strategy includes:

- **Translating organizational goals**: Ensuring that company-wide objectives are effectively broken down into team and individual goals.

- **Regular updates and check-ins**: Holding periodic meetings to track progress and address challenges.

- **Transparent communication**: Keeping employees informed about **why** specific goals matter and how they impact overall success.

An open communication culture ensures that employees remain **engaged, motivated, and accountable** for achieving business goals.

4.1.4 Foster a Culture of Accountability

When responsibilities are clearly defined, employees take **ownership of their tasks**. Assigning **goal-specific accountability** ensures that individuals know their expected contributions and outcomes.

- **Performance Reviews:** Regular assessments help track progress, identify roadblocks, and refine strategies.

- **Constructive Feedback:** Encouraging an open feedback system fosters improvement and innovation.

- **Recognition and Incentives:** Acknowledging and rewarding achievements boosts morale and motivation.

A culture of accountability ensures that goals are not just set but **actively pursued and achieved**.

4.1.5 Adaptability and Continuous Improvement

Flexibility is key in a rapidly evolving business environment. Monitoring **Key Performance Indicators (KPIs)** allows organizations to assess progress, identify inefficiencies, and make data-driven decisions.

Companies must also be prepared to **adapt goals** based on:

- **Market trends and economic shifts**

- **Competitive landscape**

- **Internal organizational changes**

By continuously evaluating and refining strategies, businesses can stay **resilient and proactive**, ensuring long-term success.

4.1.6 Empower and Motivate the Team

Involving employees in the **goal-setting process** fosters a sense of ownership and commitment. When team members contribute to defining their targets, they are more invested in achieving them.

To maintain motivation:

- **Encourage participation in decision-making**

- **Celebrate milestones and small wins.**

- **Provide growth opportunities and professional development.**

Recognizing individual and team contributions builds **a positive, high-performance culture**, driving the organization toward sustained growth.

A well-structured approach to goal-setting ensures that every individual within the organization understands their role in achieving broader business objectives. By defining **clear goals, fostering accountability, ensuring flexibility, and maintaining open communication**, businesses can **align their teams effectively and drive sustainable success**.

Setting clear goals is not just a strategy—it's a mindset that transforms **vision into action and aspirations into achievements**.

CHAPTER 5

EFFECTIVE TIME MANAGEMENT

In today's fast-paced business world, managing time effectively is more than just a useful skill—it's a strategic advantage. Many Indian businessmen face the challenge of juggling multiple responsibilities while adapting to a constantly changing market. As a chartered accountant who has seen these challenges firsthand, I believe this chapter offers practical strategies and insights to help business leaders use their time as a valuable resource. To overcome these challenges, the following suggestions and strategies can be implemented:

5.1.1 Develop a Structured Process

Effective time management is closely tied to the development of a **structured process**. By clearly outlining each step and assigning specific roles, managers ensure that time is allocated efficiently and tasks are executed with precision. This organized approach not only reduces the risk of **time wastage and errors** but also fosters accountability, enabling teams to operate seamlessly.

Regular evaluations of the time management process allow for **prompt adjustments**, ensuring that the organization remains agile and responsive to changing priorities. Such a systematic strategy transforms time from a limited resource into a **powerful asset**, driving consistent performance and overall business success.

5.1.2 Effective Implementation

Once a structured process is developed, the next step is **effective implementation**. This phase involves:

- Communicate the time management strategy clearly to all team members.

- Ensuring employees understand their specific responsibilities and the importance of timelines.

- Providing training and resources to enhance efficiency.

- Regularly monitor progress and identify challenges early on.

By making necessary **adjustments during implementation**, organizations can refine their approach, ensuring that the time management process remains effective and aligned with evolving business needs.

5.1.3 Eliminate Uncertainty

Removing uncertainties is a crucial step in ensuring clarity and smooth operations. Clear communication of **roles, responsibilities, and deadlines** minimizes misunderstandings and prevents inefficiencies. By documenting processes and expectations, management can address potential uncertainties before they escalate into larger issues.

This proactive approach strengthens accountability and fosters a work environment where each team member is **confident in their duties**, ultimately contributing to the organization's success.

5.1.4 Refinement and Reinforcement

Following the initial implementation and removal of uncertainties, organizations must conduct a **refinement phase** to ensure the process operates as intended. This phase includes:

- Monitoring the process closely.

- Gathering feedback and evaluating performance metrics.

- Identifying gaps and inefficiencies.

- Making necessary adjustments to solidify time management practices.

Adjustments and fine-tuning during this stage help create a **robust, adaptable system** that meets current needs while remaining flexible enough for future challenges. A **reinforced time management strategy** ensures consistent productivity and long-term business success.

CHAPTER 6

STREAMLINING OPERATIONS

In today's intricate regulatory landscape, Indian businesses face numerous challenges in maintaining compliance while ensuring operational efficiency. A streamlined process not only alleviates regulatory burdens but also empowers entrepreneurs to focus on growth and innovation. This chapter presents a comprehensive approach to developing, implementing, and refining operational frameworks that enhance clarity, robustness, and adaptability.

6.1.1 Developing a Framework for Each Process

A well-defined framework is the foundation of efficient operations. The process of framework development includes the following:

- **Identifying Critical Processes**: Pinpointing operations that directly impact regulatory compliance, such as financial reporting, tax filings, and internal audits.

- **Defining Objectives**: Clearly stating the goals of each process, aligning them with business strategy and regulatory requirements.

- **Mapping Roles and Responsibilities**: Assigning accountability to team members to prevent overlaps and ensure compliance adherence.

- **Establishing Performance Metrics**: Defining measurable indicators to assess efficiency and identify areas for improvement.

By systematically mapping out key activities and aligning them with compliance requirements, businesses can enhance both transparency and operational effectiveness.

6.1.2 Drafting the Process Framework

Once conceptualized, the framework must be formally documented to ensure consistency and adherence. Key elements of an effective process framework include:

- **Step-by-Step Procedures**: Clearly defined sequences of actions, including decision points, approval workflows, and contingency plans.

- **Standard Operating Procedures (SOPs)**: Comprehensive SOPs that serve as reference documents for employees, ensuring uniform execution of tasks.

- **Integration of Technology**: Leveraging digital tools for automation, document management, deadline tracking, and real-time reporting to reduce manual errors.

- **Risk Assessment and Mitigation**: Identifying potential compliance risks and embedding proactive strategies to address them.

A well-structured framework not only enhances compliance but also improves operational agility.

6.1.3 Implementation with Training

Translating a drafted framework into actionable processes requires effective implementation. This involves:

- **Clear Communication**: Ensuring all stakeholders understand their roles and the impact of the new framework through meetings and workshops.

- **Structured Training Programs**: Developing role-specific training modules covering framework nuances, new technologies, and compliance best practices.

- **Pilot Testing**: Conduct trial runs before full-scale implementation to address real-world challenges and incorporate employee feedback.

- **Feedback Mechanisms**: Establishing channels for ongoing feedback to facilitate continuous improvements.

Proper implementation ensures that employees adapt seamlessly to the new framework while maintaining compliance and efficiency.

6.1.4 Removing Complexities

The final phase focuses on simplifying the process by eliminating redundancies and inefficiencies. This involves:

- **Process Optimization**: Review each step to remove non-value-adding tasks, thereby reducing confusion and enhancing productivity.

- **Standardization**: Establishing uniform procedures across the organization to ensure consistency and ease of training for new employees.

- **Automation and Digitalization**: Minimizing manual interventions through the adoption of digital tools, thereby reducing errors and improving efficiency.

- **Continuous Improvement**: Conducting regular reviews to ensure alignment with evolving regulatory requirements and industry best practices.

By eliminating complexities, businesses can create a more agile and effective operational framework that adapts to changing regulations while promoting growth.

Key Takeaways

- A systematic framework enhances operational efficiency and regulatory compliance.

- Formal documentation, including SOPs and risk assessments, ensures clarity and uniformity.

- Effective training and feedback mechanisms drive successful implementation.

- Simplification and automation improve adaptability and long-term sustainability.

By streamlining operations, businesses can navigate regulatory landscapes with confidence while fostering innovation and scalability.

CHAPTER 7

IDENTIFYING INEFFICIENCIES IN COMPLIANCE AND REGULATORY PROCESSES, LACK OF INTERNAL AND OPERATIONAL CONTROLS

Inefficiencies can lead to financial losses, legal complications, and reputational damage for Indian businesses operating in intricate compliance and regulatory environments. This chapter outlines a structured approach to identifying, analyzing, and mitigating inefficiencies by focusing on understanding the nature of losses, detecting abnormal trends, identifying root causes, testing corrective actions, and ensuring sustainable compliance.

7.1.1 Identifying the Nature of Losses

The first step in improving operational efficiency is categorizing the types of losses businesses may face. These losses can be:

- **Financial Losses:** Due to penalties, legal fines, or inefficient resource utilization.

- **Operational Losses:** Resulting from inefficiencies, bottlenecks, or redundant processes.

- **Reputational Losses:** Stemming from non-compliance, negative media coverage, or customer dissatisfaction.

Example:

A mid-sized Indian textile exporter faced severe delays in GST filings due to manual processing errors. The resulting penalties and loss of tax benefits amounted to ₹ **five lakhs annually.** Identifying these operational inefficiencies led the company to invest in **automated tax compliance software**, which eliminated errors and reduced costs.

7.1.2 Checking for Abnormal Losses

Not all losses are routine; some indicate deeper issues. Businesses should differentiate between expected losses and abnormal losses by:

- Establishing benchmarks using historical data.

- Comparing performance against industry standards.

- Conducting periodic audits to identify deviations.

Technology Integration:

Using **AI-powered analytics tools**, businesses can **automate anomaly detection** in financial transactions, compliance adherence, and operational workflows, reducing human error and improving accuracy.

7.1.3 Identifying the Reasons for Abnormal Losses

Once abnormal losses are detected, businesses must determine their root causes. Key questions to consider:

- Are inefficiencies due to outdated processes?

- Do compliance gaps exist due to poor internal controls?

- Are external factors like regulatory changes impacting operations?

Case Study:

A logistics firm struggled with frequent customs hold-ups, delaying deliveries and increasing costs. Upon investigation, it was found that **80% of delays were due to missing regulatory documentation.** Implementing a **digital compliance tracking system** reduced errors and improved processing time.

7.1.4 Checking for Solutions and Testing

To address inefficiencies, businesses should:

- **Develop Corrective Measures:** Revise standard operating procedures, strengthen internal controls, and integrate automation.

- **Pilot Test Solutions:** Implement changes in a controlled environment before full-scale rollout.

- **Gather Feedback:** Adjust solutions based on employee input and performance data.

7.1.5 Ensuring Non-Occurrence of Future Inefficiencies

To sustain improvements, businesses should:

- Conduct **regular internal audits** and compliance checks.

- Implement **real-time monitoring dashboards** for key performance indicators.

- Foster a **culture of continuous improvement** by training employees on compliance best practices.

CHAPTER 8

AUDITING FRAMEWORK – TYPES AND BENEFITS OF AUDITS

Auditing is a cornerstone of effective business management, ensuring regulatory adherence, risk mitigation, and operational excellence.

In India's dynamic business landscape, where regulatory frameworks are continually evolving, a structured auditing approach is essential for maintaining transparency, mitigating risks, and improving financial and operational health.

This chapter provides an in-depth exploration of auditing frameworks, explaining the different types of audits, their significance, and how businesses can leverage them for long-term success.

A well-implemented audit system not only ensures adherence to statutory requirements but also helps identify inefficiencies, detect fraud, and optimize processes.

By embedding audits into the core operational strategy, businesses can drive sustained growth, enhance investor confidence, and achieve a competitive edge in the market.

8.1 Types of Audits

8.1.1 Internal Audits

An in-house team conducts internal audits to assess internal controls, risk management, and governance processes. These audits help businesses address inefficiencies before external scrutiny arises, ensuring smooth operations and compliance adherence.

8.1.2 External Audits

Independent third-party auditors carry out external audits to evaluate financial statements and regulatory compliance. They enhance credibility with stakeholders and help businesses meet statutory and industry-specific requirements, reducing the risk of penalties or legal actions.

8.1.3 Compliance Audits

Compliance audits focus on whether the organization adheres to relevant laws, regulations, and internal policies. These audits are crucial in highly regulated industries such as finance, healthcare, and manufacturing, helping businesses avoid legal repercussions and operational disruptions.

8.1.4 Operational Audits

Operational audits evaluate business processes to ensure efficiency, effectiveness, and optimal resource utilization. They help identify inefficiencies, streamline operations, and improve overall performance.

8.1.5 Forensic Audits

Forensic audits are specialized audits used to investigate fraud, embezzlement, or financial misstatements. These audits involve detailed analysis, legal considerations, and compliance checks to detect and prevent financial irregularities within an organization.

8.1.6 IT Audits

IT audits focus on evaluating the security, reliability, and efficiency of an organization's IT infrastructure. These audits assess cybersecurity risks, data protection measures, and IT governance to safeguard businesses from cyber threats and compliance violations.

8.2 Benefits of Audits

8.2.1 Enhanced Transparency and Accountability

Audits ensure that all business activities are transparent and well-documented, increasing trust among investors, regulators, and other stakeholders. Employees also become more accountable when they know their work is subject to scrutiny.

8.2.2 Improved Operational Efficiency

By identifying inefficiencies and redundant processes, audits help businesses streamline operations, reduce unnecessary costs, and enhance productivity. The insights gained facilitate data-driven decision-making, leading to smarter business practices.

8.2.3 Risk Mitigation and Compliance

Regular audits help in proactively identifying regulatory gaps, financial risks, and governance issues, allowing businesses to take corrective actions before problems escalate. This minimizes legal penalties and operational disruptions.

8.2.4 Strategic Planning and Continuous Improvement

Audit reports provide valuable insights that aid in long-term strategic planning and continuous improvement initiatives. Organizations can use these findings to refine business models, optimize financial planning, and implement best practices for sustained growth.

8.2.5 Increased Stakeholder Confidence

Audits reassure investors, creditors, and customers that the business is financially sound, well-managed, and compliant with regulatory standards. This increases credibility and opens doors for better investment and business opportunities.

8.2.6 Fraud Prevention and Detection

Forensic and compliance audits help in detecting fraudulent activities within an organization. Early identification of financial misconduct ensures that appropriate legal action can be taken, preventing further financial loss.

8.2.7 Strengthened IT Security

With increasing cyber threats, IT audits play a crucial role in safeguarding business data and ensuring compliance with data protection regulations. These audits help businesses adopt robust cybersecurity measures and avoid potential cyber risks.

Example:

An Indian pharmaceutical company undergoing an **unexpected regulatory audit** discovered gaps in its quality control procedures. By implementing **automated compliance tracking**, they avoided future penalties and secured better investment opportunities.

Conclusion:

By integrating robust auditing practices and leveraging technology, Indian businesses can **minimize inefficiencies, ensure compliance, and enhance overall sustainability.** A well-structured audit framework strengthens governance, improves decision-making, and ensures business continuity in an ever-evolving regulatory landscape.

CHAPTER 9

CUSTOMER RELATIONSHIP MANAGEMENT

In today's competitive business landscape, building and maintaining customer loyalty is essential for long-term success. A strong customer relationship management (CRM) strategy not only fosters repeat business but also turns satisfied customers into brand advocates. With the rise of digital transformation and evolving customer expectations, businesses must adopt data-driven CRM strategies to ensure customer retention and loyalty. This chapter outlines effective strategies for developing robust CRM practices, especially for Indian entrepreneurs facing complex market challenges.

9.1.1. Building a Customer-Centric Approach

A customer-centric culture begins with understanding clients' needs, preferences, and expectations. Businesses should invest in market research and customer feedback systems to gather insights that inform personalized strategies. By aligning products and services with customer expectations, organizations can create a strong emotional connection that underpins loyalty.

Additionally, cultural nuances in India, such as personalized service and trust-based relationships, play a significant role in fostering long-term customer engagement. Companies like **Zomato and Flipkart** leverage localized strategies to enhance customer experience, demonstrating the importance of understanding regional preferences.

9.1.2. Developing an Effective CRM Framework

A structured CRM framework is the backbone of successful customer management. Key elements include:

- **Data Collection and Analysis:** Leverage technology to capture customer data across various touchpoints, such as purchase history, feedback, and online interactions. AI-driven CRM tools help identify patterns and trends that inform targeted engagement strategies.

- **Segmentation:** Divide the customer base into distinct groups based on behavior, demographics, or purchasing patterns. Tailored communication and offers ensure that each segment feels valued and understood.

- **Integrated Systems:** Implement CRM software that consolidates customer interactions across channels. This integration enables a seamless experience, whether customers engage online, in-store, or via customer service.

9.1.3. Strategies for Enhancing Customer Engagement

Effective engagement is crucial for fostering loyalty. Entrepreneurs can adopt several strategies, including:

- **Personalized Communication:** Use customer data to tailor messages and offers. Personalized emails, targeted promotions, and loyalty programs help build a deeper connection.

- **Proactive Service:** Anticipate customer needs and address potential issues before they escalate. Regular follow-ups and prompt responses to inquiries create a sense of care and reliability.

- **Multi-Channel Interaction:** Ensure consistency in communication by utilizing various channels such as social media, mobile apps, and customer service centers. A cohesive multi-channel strategy ensures customers receive a unified brand experience.

- **Social Listening:** Monitor brand mentions on social media to understand customer sentiments and address concerns in real-time.

- **Community Engagement:** In India, customer loyalty often strengthens through **localized engagement**, such as WhatsApp groups for updates and customer support or loyalty clubs offering exclusive benefits.

9.1.4. Monitoring and Measuring Loyalty

To maintain long-term customer relationships, it is important to monitor loyalty metrics and adjust strategies accordingly continuously:

- **Customer Satisfaction Surveys:** Regularly conduct surveys to gauge satisfaction levels and gather actionable insights.

- **Net Promoter Score (NPS):** Use NPS as an indicator of customer loyalty and willingness to recommend the brand.

- **Retention Rates:** Track the percentage of repeat customers over time to assess the effectiveness of CRM initiatives.

- **Engagement Metrics:** Monitor social media interactions, email open rates, and response times to measure engagement effectiveness.

9.1.5. Continuous Improvement and Adaptation

Customer needs and market dynamics are ever-changing. A commitment to continuous improvement is key to sustaining loyalty. Businesses should:

- **Review Feedback:** Regularly analyze customer feedback to identify areas for improvement.

- **Update CRM Strategies:** Adapt communication and engagement strategies based on emerging trends and evolving customer preferences.

- **Invest in Training:** Equip employees with the latest CRM practices and tools to ensure they can effectively manage customer relationships.

- **Leverage AI and Automation:** AI-driven chatbots and predictive analytics can streamline customer support and improve response efficiency.

Conclusion

A well-executed CRM strategy is fundamental to business growth. By understanding customer preferences, leveraging technology, and maintaining proactive engagement, businesses can ensure long-term success. For Indian entrepreneurs, balancing technological advancements with culturally relevant customer interactions is the key to sustainable customer relationships.

Implementing and refining CRM strategies continuously will help businesses retain customers and turn them into passionate brand advocates.

CHAPTER 10

SCALING BUSINESS PRACTICES

Scaling a business requires a strategic and systematic approach to expanding operations, reaching new markets, and increasing revenue—all while maintaining operational excellence and compliance. For Indian entrepreneurs facing a competitive and complex regulatory environment, adopting scalable practices is essential for long-term growth. This chapter outlines key strategies and best practices for scaling business operations effectively.

10.1.1. Strategic Planning and Vision

Scaling begins with a clear vision and a robust strategic plan. Business leaders must define long-term goals and map out a detailed roadmap for growth. This involves:

- **Market Analysis:** Assessing market trends, customer needs, and competitive landscapes.

- **Goal Setting:** Establishing specific, measurable objectives that align with the overall business strategy.

- **Risk Management:** Identifying potential challenges and developing contingency plans to mitigate risks.

10.1.2. Process Optimization and Standardization

Efficient processes form the backbone of scalability. Streamlining operations ensures that the business can handle increased demand without compromising quality or compliance. Key steps include:

- **Documenting Processes:** Creating detailed Standard Operating Procedures (SOPs) for all critical functions.

- **Eliminating Inefficiencies:** Regularly reviewing workflows to remove redundancies and improve productivity.

- **Leveraging Technology:** Automating routine tasks with digital tools to maintain consistency and reduce manual errors.

10.1.3. Technology Adoption and Digital Transformation

Technology is a powerful enabler for scaling business practices. Embracing digital transformation can enhance efficiency, facilitate communication, and improve data-driven decision-making. Consider:

- **Implementing ERP Systems:** Integrating enterprise resource planning software to streamline operations across various departments.

- **Data Analytics:** Utilizing analytics tools to monitor performance, understand customer behavior, and identify growth opportunities.

- **Cloud Solutions:** Migrating to cloud-based platforms for scalable and flexible infrastructure that supports business expansion.

10.1.4. Talent Management and Organizational Culture

A dynamic and skilled workforce supports a scalable business. Investing in talent and fostering a culture of continuous improvement are crucial for sustainable growth:

- **Hiring Strategically:** Attracting and retaining skilled professionals who can drive innovation and manage increased workloads.

- **Training and Development:** Providing regular training to equip employees with the necessary skills and knowledge to adapt to new systems and processes.

- **Empowering Teams:** Encouraging a culture of collaboration and accountability where employees are motivated to contribute to the company's success.

10.1.5. Financial Management and Investment

Scaling operations often require additional financial resources. Effective financial planning and management are vital to ensure that the business can sustain its growth trajectory:

- **Budgeting and Forecasting:** Developing realistic financial projections that account for increased operational costs and revenue growth.

- **Securing Funding:** Exploring various financing options such as equity funding, loans, or government grants to support expansion initiatives.

- **Cost Control:** Implementing robust cost management practices to ensure efficient use of resources and protect profit margins.

10.1.6. Monitoring, Feedback, and Continuous Improvement

As the business scales, it is essential to monitor performance and refine strategies based on real-time feedback continuously:

- **Performance Metrics:** Establishing Key Performance Indicators (KPIs) that track progress across different business functions.

- **Regular Reviews:** Conducting periodic performance evaluations to identify areas for improvement and adjust strategies accordingly.

- **Feedback Loops:** Encouraging input from employees, customers, and stakeholders to drive continuous process enhancement.

CHAPTER 11

COMPREHENSIVE COMPLIANCE AND REGULATORY MANAGEMENT FOR INDIAN BUSINESSES

In India's rapidly evolving business landscape, maintaining stringent compliance with regulatory requirements is a critical pillar for success. Businesses across various structures—proprietorships, partnerships, LLPs, and public or private companies—must navigate an intricate web of laws and guidelines that, if not adhered to, can result in severe penalties, operational disruptions, and long-term reputational damage. This chapter presents a detailed exploration of each facet of compliance, the common mistakes that lead to non-compliance, the hefty penalties incurred, and strategic solutions to mitigate these risks. The goal is to equip Indian entrepreneurs with the knowledge and tools needed to establish robust compliance frameworks and avoid pitfalls that can jeopardize their operations.

11.1 Understanding Compliance Requirements Based on Business Structure

The regulatory framework in India is multifaceted, with requirements that differ significantly based on a business's legal structure. A deep understanding of these requirements is the cornerstone of effective compliance management.

11.1.1 Proprietorship

Overview:

A proprietorship is the simplest form of business entity, typically owned and managed by a single individual.

Although it benefits from fewer regulatory formalities compared to other structures, the proprietor is personally liable for all business obligations.

Key Compliance Requirements:

- **Trade Name Registration:**

  Registration with local authorities ensures that the business name is recognized legally.

- **Income Tax Filings:**

  Income is reported as personal income on the proprietor's tax returns. The process must align with the prevailing tax rules and regulations.

- **GST Registration:**

  Mandatory if the annual turnover exceeds the specified threshold. Regular GST returns (monthly or quarterly) are required.

- **Record-Keeping:**

- Maintaining accurate financial records is essential to support all filings and claims.

Common Pitfalls:

- **Delayed Registrations:** Often, proprietors neglect timely registration, leading to complications in tax filings.

- **Inadequate Documentation:** Poor record-keeping results in miscalculations, errors in tax returns, and subsequent penalties.

Impact of Non-Compliance:

- **Financial Penalties:** Fines for late tax filings and GST submissions can compound over time, impacting liquidity.

- **Operational Risks:** The absence of proper documentation can hinder business credibility and future financing options.

11.1.2 Partnership Firm

Overview:

Two or more individuals form partnership firms. While they share profits, they also share liabilities, making joint compliance critical.

Key Compliance Requirements:

- **Partnership Deed Registration:**

  A legally binding document that outlines roles, profit-sharing ratios, and dispute resolution mechanisms.

- **Income Tax Filings:**

  Both the firm and the individual partners must file their tax returns.

- **GST Compliance:**

  Required once the firm's turnover surpasses the threshold, similar to proprietorships.

- **Financial Records:**

  Consolidated accounts must be maintained to reflect the partnership's operations accurately.

Common Pitfalls:

- **Poor Communication:** Disjointed efforts among partners often lead to delayed or erroneous filings.

- **Inconsistent Record-Keeping:** Varying standards of financial management can create discrepancies, leading to compliance failures.

Impact of Non-Compliance:

- **Hefty Fines:** Failure to file returns on time can attract substantial fines, affecting the firm's profitability.

- **Legal Disputes:** Inconsistencies in financial documentation may trigger disputes among partners, escalating to legal conflicts.

11.1.3 Limited Liability Partnership (LLP)

Overview:

LLPs combine the operational flexibility of a partnership with the limited liability benefits of a company. They are subject to stricter regulatory norms than proprietorships or traditional partnerships.

Key Compliance Requirements:

- **LLP Agreement Registration:**

  This document must detail the responsibilities and profit-sharing among partners.

- **Annual Filings with MCA:**

  LLPs are required to file the Statement of Accounts and Solvency within 60 days after the close of the financial year.

- **Tax and GST Returns:**

  Similar compliance obligations exist as in other business forms, with strict deadlines.

Common Pitfalls:

- **Failure to Update Agreements:** Changes in business operations are often not reflected in the LLP agreement, leading to outdated compliance information.

- **Delayed MCA Filings:** Overlooking the statutory deadline for MCA submissions is a frequent oversight.

Impact of Non-Compliance:

- **Statutory Fines:** Non-adherence to MCA filing deadlines can result in significant monetary penalties.

- **Regulatory Intervention:** Repeated lapses may invite closer scrutiny from regulatory bodies, increasing the likelihood of audits and investigations.

11.1.4 Private and Public Limited Companies

Overview:

These companies are the most complex in terms of regulatory requirements, involving rigorous documentation, frequent audits, and multi-layered compliance obligations.

Key Compliance Requirements:

- **Incorporation and Statutory Filings:**

  Companies must regularly update their incorporation documents, file annual returns, and communicate any structural changes to the MCA.

- **Board and General Meetings:**

  Regular meetings are mandated under the Companies Act, with precise record-keeping of minutes and resolutions.

- **Financial Reporting and Audits:**

  Comprehensive and audited financial statements must be prepared in accordance with applicable accounting standards.

- **Tax, GST, TDS, and Other Statutory Compliances:**

  Compliance extends to labor laws, environmental regulations, and industry-specific requirements.

- **Record-Keeping and Documentation:**

  Maintaining extensive records is crucial for audit purposes and to support all statutory filings.

Common Pitfalls:

- **Non-Adherence to Meeting Protocols:** Failure to conduct timely board and general meetings can result in regulatory non-compliance.

- **Complex Financial Reporting:** Misinterpretation of accounting standards often leads to errors in audited accounts.

- **Overlooking Minor Filings:** In a complex regulatory framework, even minor filings (such as changes in shareholding or director appointments) can be overlooked.

Impact of Non-Compliance:

- **Severe Financial Fines:** Non-compliance can attract significant fines that drain financial resources and tarnish the company's reputation.

- **Legal Repercussions:** In extreme cases, non-compliance may result in legal actions against company officials, including criminal proceedings.

- **Investor Confidence:** Persistent compliance issues can deter investors and lead to a loss in market value.

11.2. Hefty Penalties and Their Impact on Business

Non-compliance in India is not a trivial matter; it has far-reaching consequences that can jeopardize a business's survival. Below are detailed insights into the different types of penalties and their impacts.

11.2.1 Financial Penalties

- **Late Filing Fees:**

  Each day of delay in filing returns—be it income tax, GST, or MCA submissions—results in fines that accumulate over time. For large corporations, these fines can reach astronomical figures.

- **Interest Charges:**

  Outstanding taxes accrue interest, significantly increasing the financial burden. This not only affects cash flow but can also reduce profitability.

- **Statutory Fines:**

  Specific non-compliance issues, such as inaccurate disclosures or failure to maintain proper records, can lead to hefty fines as per the applicable statutes.

- **Loss of Incentives:**

  Non-compliance can result in the forfeiture of tax benefits, deductions, or other incentives designed to promote business growth.

11.2.2 Operational Disruptions

- **Suspension of Operations:** Regulatory bodies have the authority to suspend business licenses or halt operations until compliance is restored, leading to revenue loss and operational chaos.

- **Increased Audits and Inspections:**

A record of non-compliance often triggers more frequent audits, which divert management focus and resources from core business activities.

- **Resource Diversion:**

Time and resources that could be used for business development are instead spent on rectifying compliance issues and handling legal disputes.

11.2.3 Legal and Reputational Consequences

- **Litigation and Criminal Prosecution:**

In cases of chronic non-compliance, regulatory bodies may initiate legal proceedings that could result in criminal charges against the company's directors or responsible officers.

- **Reputational Damage:**

News of regulatory violations spreads quickly, leading to a loss of stakeholder trust. This affects not only current business operations but also future growth prospects, as investors and customers tend to shy away from companies with tarnished reputations.

11.3. Critical Mistakes Made by Businessmen

Understanding where businesses typically falter in compliance management is key to developing a proactive strategy. Here are some of the most critical mistakes:

11.3.1 Inadequate Record-Keeping

- **Lack of Comprehensive Documentation:**

  Inadequate or disorganized records lead to errors during audits and tax filings. This includes failure to systematically maintain invoices, receipts, bank statements, and contracts.

- **Reliance on Manual Processes:**

  Manual record-keeping is prone to errors and often results in lost data, miscalculations, and delays in filing statutory returns.

11.3.2 Delayed or Missed Filings

- **Failure to Track Deadlines:**

  Business owners frequently lose track of multiple filing deadlines, which vary based on the type of compliance. Missing these deadlines can result in substantial fines.

- **Procrastination in Gathering Required Documents:**

  Delays in compiling financial statements and supporting documents lead to rushed filings, increasing the risk of errors.

11.3.3 Poor Coordination and Communication

- **Fragmented Responsibilities:**

  In multi-partner or large corporate structures, the lack of clear accountability and communication often results in overlapping responsibilities and missed compliance tasks.

- **Ineffective Internal Controls:**

  Without strong internal controls, errors go unnoticed, and compliance lapses occur more frequently.

11.3.4 Inability to Adapt to Regulatory Changes

- **Outdated Procedures:**

  Regulatory frameworks are dynamic, and failure to update internal processes can result in non-compliance. Business owners often rely on legacy systems and are slow to adopt new regulatory practices.

- **Lack of Continuous Training:**

  Employees and management must be regularly trained on new compliance requirements. A failure to invest in training is a recurring mistake that leads to systemic non-compliance.

11.3.5 Misinterpretation of Complex Regulations

- **Over-Simplification of Guidelines:**

  Regulations are often complex, and an oversimplified interpretation can result in filing errors or non-compliance with certain clauses.

- **Lack of Expert Consultation:**

  Many businessmen attempt to handle compliance internally without seeking expert advice, which leads to misinterpretation and subsequent mistakes.

11.4. Strategic Solutions and the Role of Professional Chartered Accountant Firms

Engaging professional expertise is essential to counteracting these challenges and mitigating the impact of non-compliance. Chartered accountant firms offer a comprehensive suite of services designed to streamline compliance processes and safeguard businesses against regulatory risks.

11.4.1 Expert Advisory and Consultation

- **Regulatory Mapping and Analysis:**

  Expert firms conduct thorough analyses of the regulatory landscape relevant to your business structure. They provide a detailed map of all compliance requirements, ensuring nothing is overlooked.

- **Tailored Compliance Strategies:**

  Customized solutions are developed based on the unique needs of the business, incorporating industry-specific guidelines and best practices.

- **Regular Updates and Alerts:**

  Continuous monitoring of regulatory changes allows these professionals to provide timely updates and alerts, ensuring that businesses remain compliant in a dynamic environment.

11.4.2 Implementation of Robust Internal Controls

- **Automated Systems:**

  Utilizing modern accounting and compliance software, chartered accountant firms implement automated systems to track deadlines, manage records, and prepare accurate filings.

- **Internal Audits and Reviews:**

  Regular internal audits are scheduled to review compliance processes, identify gaps, and implement corrective actions before issues escalate.

- **Comprehensive Checklists and SOPs:**

  Detailed standard operating procedures (SOPs) and checklists are implemented, ensuring that every compliance task is executed accurately and on time.

11.4.3 Training and Capacity Building

- **Employee Training Programs:**

  Regular training sessions are organized to keep employees updated on the latest compliance requirements and internal processes.

- **Workshops and Seminars:**

  Expert-led workshops help in understanding the nuances of regulatory changes and the practical steps needed to ensure adherence.

- **Continuous Professional Development:**

  Encouraging and facilitating professional development for key compliance personnel ensures that the organization remains proactive rather than reactive.

11.4.4 Risk Mitigation and Continuous Monitoring

- **Proactive Compliance Calendar:**

  A detailed calendar of all statutory deadlines and internal review dates is maintained. Compliance professionals regularly update and review this calendar.

- **Ongoing Monitoring:**

  Continuous monitoring mechanisms are implemented to identify potential issues early. Automated alerts and periodic reviews help in maintaining compliance without lapses.

- **Feedback and Improvement Mechanisms:**

  Structured feedback channels are established to gather insights from employees and auditors, enabling continuous refinement of compliance practices.

11.5. Strategic Recommendations for Sustainable Compliance Management

To build a resilient compliance framework, businesses should adopt a proactive, strategic approach that incorporates the following key elements:

11.5.1 Develop and Implement a Comprehensive Compliance Framework

- **Regulatory Mapping:**

  Based on the business structure, identify all applicable laws and regulations. Document each requirement and establish clear responsibilities for compliance.

- **SOPs and Checklists:**

  Create detailed standard operating procedures and checklists for each compliance activity, ensuring consistency across the organization.

- **Integrated Systems:**

  Leverage digital tools to integrate compliance management with daily operations, facilitating real-time monitoring and reporting.

11.5.2 Establish a Culture of Compliance

- **Leadership Commitment:**

  Senior management must lead by example and demonstrate a strong commitment to compliance. This sets the tone for the entire organization.

- **Transparent Communication:**

  Foster an environment where compliance issues can be discussed openly and corrective actions are implemented without delay.

- **Accountability:**

- Clearly delineate roles and responsibilities, holding individuals accountable for their compliance obligations.

11.5.3 Invest in Continuous Training and Capacity Building

- **Regular Training Sessions:**

  Schedule periodic training sessions for employees at all levels to ensure they understand and adhere to compliance requirements.

- **Workshops with Experts:**

  Organize seminars and workshops with industry experts to discuss emerging trends and best practices in compliance.

- **Performance Metrics:**

  Implement key performance indicators (KPIs) to measure the effectiveness of compliance initiatives and drive continuous improvement.

11.5.4 Proactive Monitoring and Internal Auditing

- **Scheduled Audits:**

  Regular internal audits are essential to assess compliance, identify weaknesses, and implement corrective actions before issues become critical.

- **Automated Alerts:**

  Use technology to set up automated alerts for upcoming deadlines and regulatory changes.

- **Feedback Mechanisms:**

  Establish robust channels for feedback to refine and improve the compliance framework continually.

11.6. Conclusion

Effective compliance and regulatory management are essential for the long-term sustainability and success of Indian businesses. As explored in this chapter, understanding the unique compliance requirements based on the business structure, recognizing critical mistakes, and appreciating the severe financial, operational, legal, and reputational penalties of non-compliance are crucial steps in developing a resilient business. By engaging professional chartered accountant firms and implementing robust internal controls, businesses can not only avoid costly penalties but also build a strong foundation of trust and operational excellence.

A proactive and comprehensive compliance framework—bolstered by continuous training, automated systems, and regular internal audits—ensures that businesses can navigate the complexities of India's regulatory environment with confidence. The investment in proper compliance management is not merely a legal necessity but a strategic imperative that protects and enhances the overall value of the organization.

In summary, the pathway to sustainable growth lies in anticipating challenges, addressing common pitfalls, and leveraging expert guidance to create a culture of compliance. This approach not only safeguards the business against heavy penalties and operational disruptions but also positions it as a trusted and reliable player in a competitive market.

Schedule of Statutory Compliances

The following tables provide a detailed schedule of statutory compliance requirements based on the latest enacted laws, including provisions under PF & ESIC regulations, the Companies Act, the Income Tax Act, and the GST Act. This schedule outlines the key due dates and essential details for each compliance requirement, serving as a practical reference for ensuring that all statutory obligations are met in a timely manner. Readers are encouraged to regularly review these deadlines and consult with qualified professionals or legal experts to confirm current requirements before taking any action.

PF & ESIC Compliance

Compliance Requirement	Due Date	Details
PF Dues, Pension & Insurance Fund Contributions	Remit by the 15th of the following month	Overall, PF & ESIC dues must be paid by the 15th of every month
Submission of Employee Details	Within 1 month	Details of employees enrolled in the PF fund
Submission of Nomination Form	Immediately upon joining	To be submitted in the prescribed form
Reporting Additions of Members	Within 15 days of the following month	Report newly enrolled members
Reporting Deletions of Members	By the 21st of the following month	Report members who leave
Submission of Detailed Contribution Information	By the 25th of the following month	Provide a breakdown of employee and employer contributions
Submission of Annual Wage & Contribution Details	By 30th April annually	Annual submission of wages and contributions
Filing of Yearly Consolidated Statement (Form 3A)	Annually	File the consolidated statement with Form 3A

Companies Act Compliance

Compliance Requirement	Due Date / Frequency	Details
Disclosure of Director Interests (MBP-1)	At the first board meeting of each financial year	Directors must disclose interests and update promptly upon any changes
Filing of Annual Director Disclosure (DIR-8)	Annually	File non-disqualification disclosures using the prescribed form
Filing of Annual Return (MGT-7)	Within 60 days after the AGM	Annual Return for the period 1st April to 31st March
Submission of Financial Statements (AOC-4 via E-form)	Annually	Includes Balance Sheet, Profit & Loss Account, Directors' Report, Auditor's Report, etc.
Board Meetings	Minimum 4 per year (no gap exceeding 120 days)	Regular board meetings are mandatory
Holding the AGM	Within 15 months of the previous meeting (or within 6 months post-FY)	For subsequent AGMs; first AGM within 9 months from FY closure
Additional Filings (DPT-3, DIR-3 KYC)	Annually (DIR-3 KYC by 30th September)	Other mandatory filings under the Companies Act

Income Tax Act Compliance

Compliance Requirement	Due Date / Frequency	Details
Advance Tax Payment	Quarterly (15th of June, September, December, and March)	Payment of advance tax as prescribed
Filing of Income Tax Return	Annually	File the return of income as prescribed with different due dates applicable to the different assessee and depending on the applicability of tax audit #
Remittance of TDS Payments (Salary & Non-Salary)	Monthly (by 7th of the following month; March due by 30th April)	Timely remittance of withheld taxes
Filing of TDS Returns	Quarterly (31st July, 31st October, 31st January, 31st May)	Quarterly filing for TDS returns
Issuance of TDS Certificates (Form 16A – Non-Salary)	Quarterly (15th day of August, November, February, and June)	Issue TDS certificates for non-salary payments

Issuance of Salary TDS Certificate (Form 16)	Annually (by 15th June of the following financial year)	Issue the salary TDS certificate
Filing of Tax Audit (Form 3CD with Form 3CB)	Annually (by 30th September)	File audit details as per prescribed guidelines
Filing of Form 61A	Annually (by 31st May)	File for specified financial transactions

Note: A tax audit becomes compulsory if a business's gross turnover exceeds Rs. 1 crore in the preceding financial year. The threshold limit will be increased to Rs. 10 crores if the cash transactions do not exceed 5% of total transactions.

GST Act Compliance

Compliance Requirement	Due Date / Frequency	Details
Filing of GSTR-1	Monthly (for turnover > ₹1.5 Cr) or Quarterly (for turnover < ₹1.5 Cr)	Returns due on the 11th day of the succeeding month (monthly) or by 13th of month following the quarter.

Filing of GSTR-3B (Discharge of GSTR Dues and Return under QRMP)	Monthly (by 20th of every month)	File the return monthly (Applicable to Monthly Filers). In the QRMP scheme, the taxpayer files GSTR-3B on a quarterly basis and pays tax every month.
Filing of Return for Input Service Distributors (GSTR-6)	Monthly (by the 13th of the succeeding month)	Applicable for registered input service distributors
Filing of Annual Return (GSTR-9) and Reconciliation Statement (GSTR-9C, if applicable)	Annually (by 31st December following the end of the financial year)	Annual return (GSTR-9) is applicable if Aggregate turnover exceeds 2 crore, and Reconciliation Statement GSTR9C is applicable if aggregate turnover ≥ ₹2 Crore

DISCLAIMER

The information provided in the above compliance schedule is based on current statutory provisions and is subject to change without prior notice.

The author assumes no liability for any loss or damage incurred by readers who rely on this information. It is strongly recommended that you consult with qualified professionals or legal experts before taking any action based on these schedules.

Please note that the above compliance schedule is generally applicable; however, additional compliance requirements may apply depending on your specific business structure and circumstances.

Always seek personalized advice from a professional to ensure full adherence to all relevant laws and regulations.

Final Thoughts

"Compliance is more than a legal obligation—it is a strategic advantage that fosters trust, stability, and long-term success. While this book provides a structured compliance framework, it is important to recognize that regulations evolve, and each business has unique requirements. Staying informed, maintaining accurate records, and consulting professionals will ensure that your business remains on the right side of the law.

A proactive approach to compliance not only minimizes risks but also strengthens credibility and operational efficiency. By making compliance an integral part of your business strategy, you safeguard your organization's future and create a foundation for sustainable growth. Remember, compliance is not just about meeting legal requirements—it's about building a responsible, resilient, and thriving business. Stay informed, stay prepared, and stay ahead."

Mohit Makkar

(Practicing Chartered Accountant & Author)